Tinwhistle for Beginners

by

Dona Gilliam & Mizzy McCaskill

HISTORY OF THE TINWHISTLE

Once upon a time six-holed whistles were made of tin and sold in the British Isles for a penny. As tradition would have it they were named for these traits, and today our small friend is called the pennywhistle or tinwhistle.

*To do a great thing well
one must first do the simplest things perfectly.*

Fingering Chart

○ **open hole**
● **closed hole**

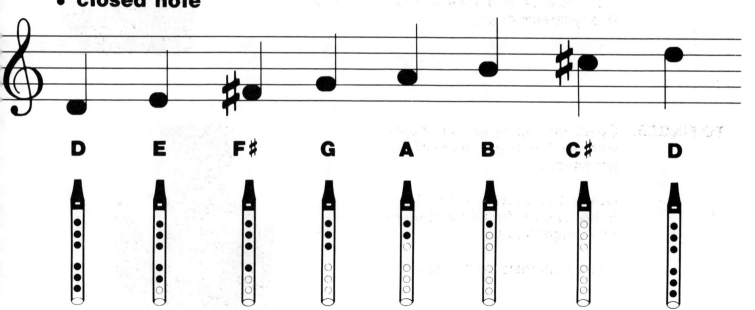

TO BEGIN: Hold the whistle with right hand around the bottom.
Place the mouthpiece between the lips.

Sit up straight. Take a normal breath.
Move tongue as if saying "too" while blowing a steady stream of air.

TO FINGER: Cover the top three tone holes with the first three fingers of the left hand.

Cover the bottom three tone holes with the first three fingers of the right hand.

Instrument rests on thumbs.

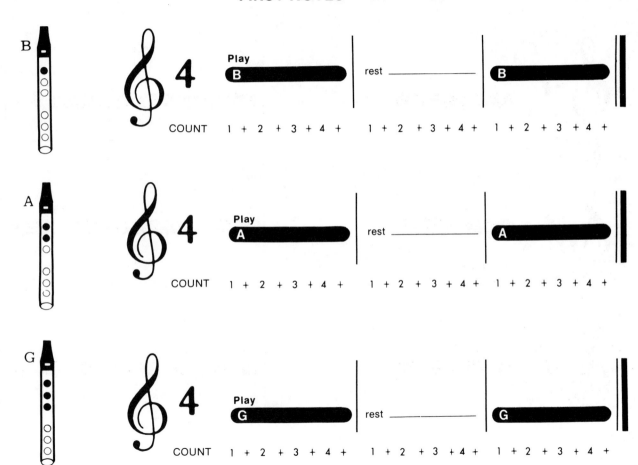

6

TONGUING EXERCISE

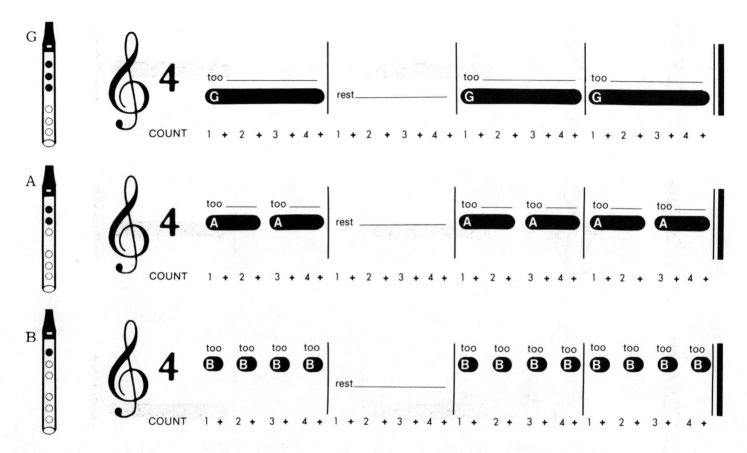

TRIO

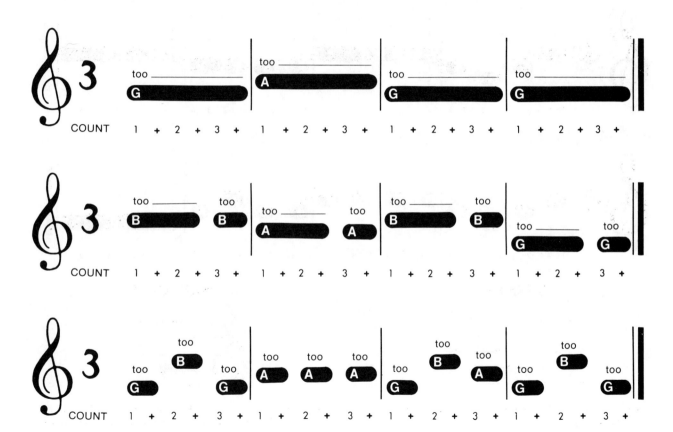

MERRILY WE ROLL ALONG

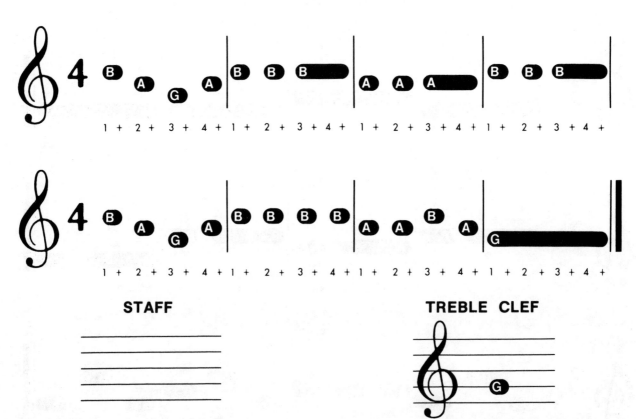

STAFF

The STAFF consists of five lines and four spaces on which notes are placed.

TREBLE CLEF

A TREBLE CLEF or G-CLEF is placed at the beginning of a staff. It indicates the pitch of the notes to follow because it circles the G line.

MUSICAL FACTS

BAR LINE — **Bar lines** are used to divide the staff into measures.

MEASURE — The space between two bar lines is called a **Measure.**

DOUBLE BAR LINE — The **Double Bar line** is used at the end of a musical selection.

TIME SIGNATURE

$$\frac{4}{4}, \frac{3}{4}, \frac{2}{4}$$

Top number tells how many counts in a measure

Bottom number tells what kind of note receives one count (1/4, ♩, or one quarter note)

FOLK SONG DUET

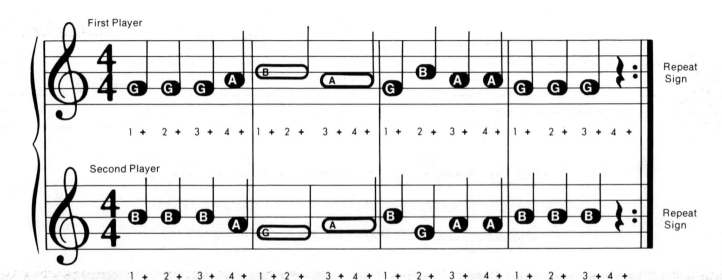

REPEAT SIGNS

REPEAT SIGNS indicate that music between the two signs is to be repeated. If only one repeat sign is used return to the beginning.

QUARTER REST

The QUARTER REST receives one count.

HOT CROSS BUNS

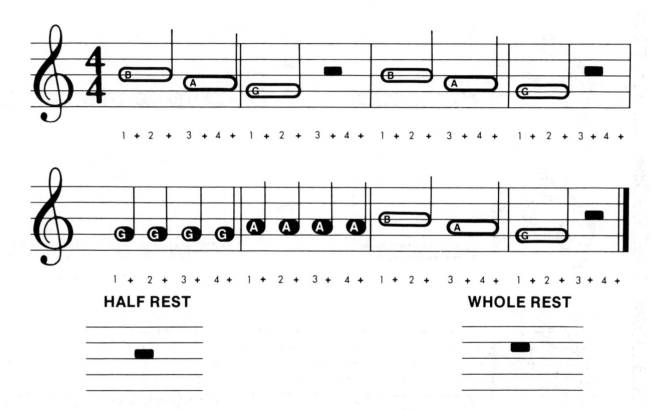

HALF REST

The HALF REST receives two counts. Notice that it sits on a line.

WHOLE REST

The WHOLE REST receives four counts. Notice that it hangs from a line.

NEW NOTES

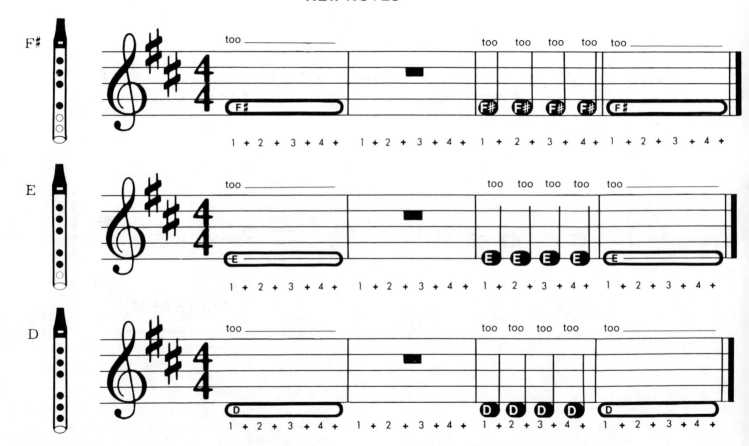

LIGHTLY ROW

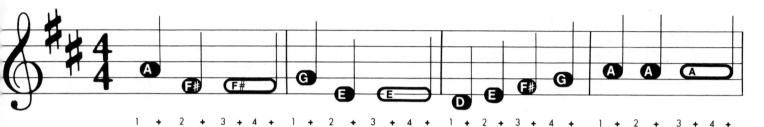

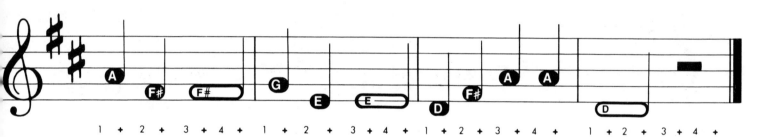

KEY SIGNATURE

The Pocket Companion is an instrument pitched in the key of D (when all of the tone holes are covered, the note D sounds). The key of D has two sharps: F sharp and C sharp. (# - symbol for sharp)

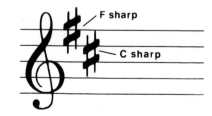

TWINKLE TWINKLE LITTLE STAR

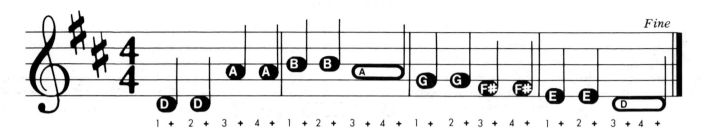

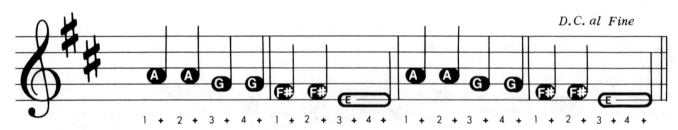

D.C. al Fine — Da Capo al Fine means to repeat from the beginning to a place marked Fine.

NOTE NAMES

SPACES

Spells: **F A C E**

LINES

Spells: **Every Good Boy Does Fine**

LONDON BRIDGE

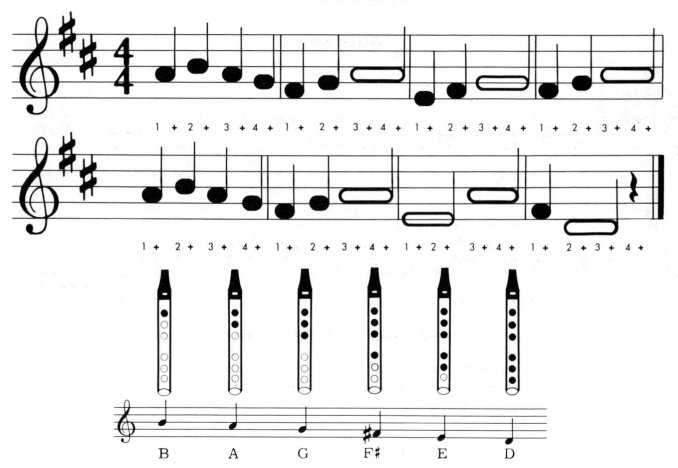

16

JINGLE BELLS

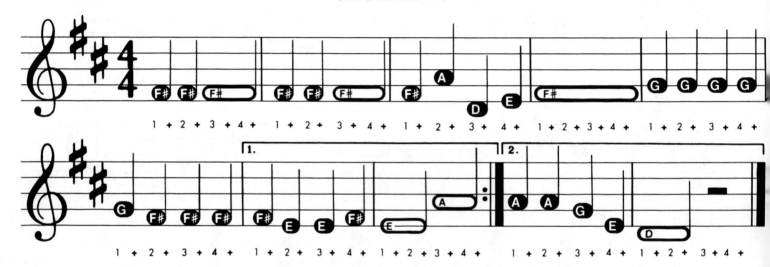

FIRST AND SECOND ENDINGS

FIRST ENDING

> **1.**
> Play first time only

SECOND ENDING

> **2.**
> Play second time only

HICKORY DICKORY DOCK

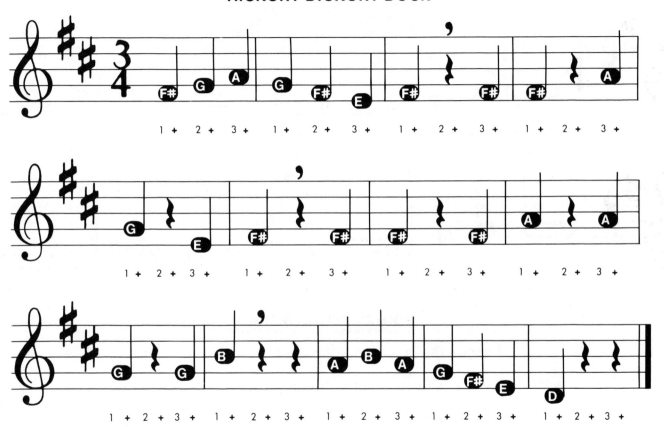

' A BREATH MARK indicates the proper place to breathe when playing.

GO TELL AUNT RHODY

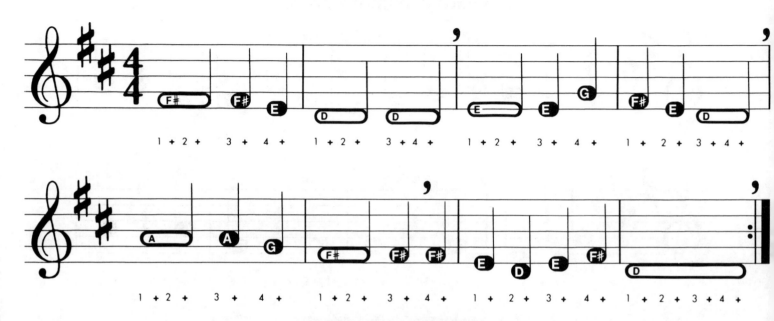

POINTS TO REMEMBER:

1. Tongue the beginning of each note as if saying "too".

2. Blow a slow, gentle air stream.

3. Cover the tone holes completely for the notes to sound.

Here is a piece beginning on the last count of the measure.

This note is called a pick-up note.

A TISKET, A TASKET

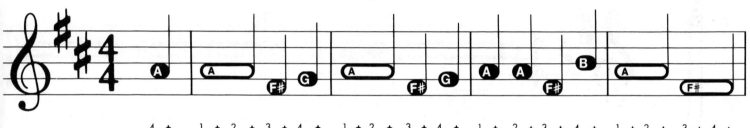

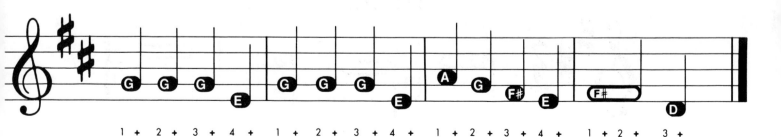

20

High
D

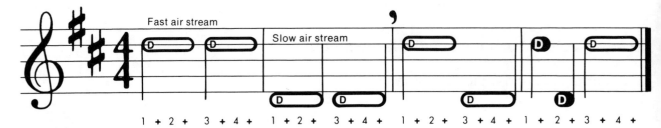

Fast air stream

Slow air stream

1 + 2 + 3 + 4 + 1 + 2 + 3 + 4 + 1 + 2 + 3 + 4 + 1 + 2 + 3 + 4 +

C♯

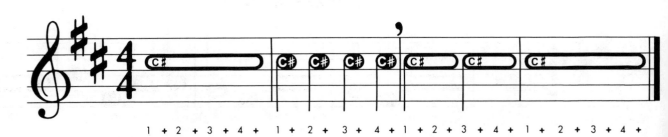

1 + 2 + 3 + 4 + 1 + 2 + 3 + 4 + 1 + 2 + 3 + 4 + 1 + 2 + 3 + 4 +

EXERCISE

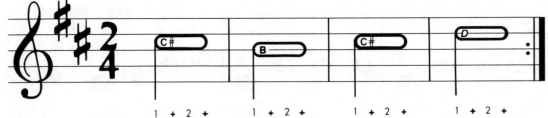

1 + 2 +   1 + 2 +   1 + 2 +   1 + 2 +

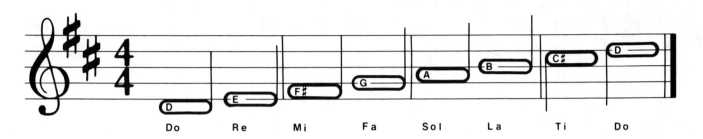

SCALE EXERCISE

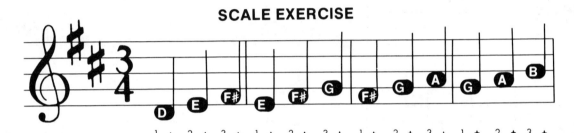

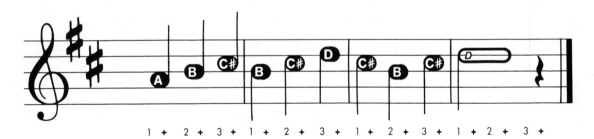

DUET

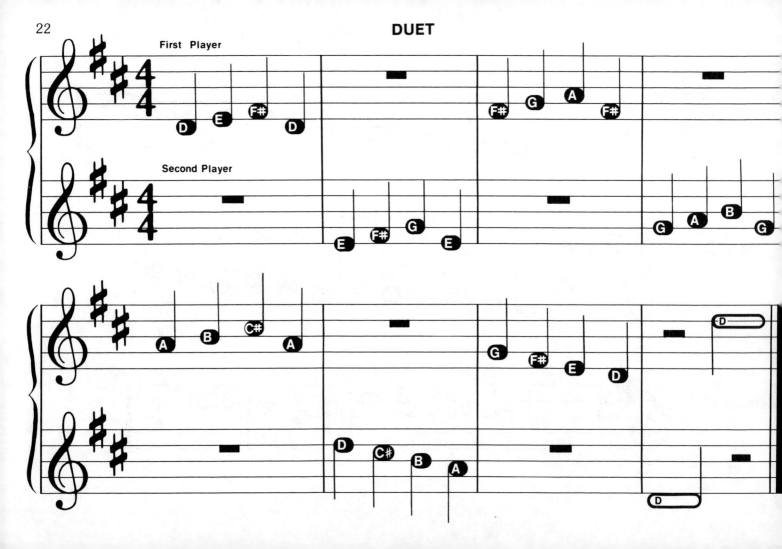

A ROUND is a song in which two or more groups play the same melody starting at different times.

23

ALLEGRO (Round)

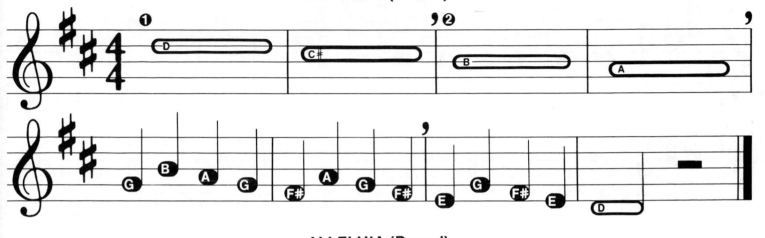

ALLELUIA (Round)

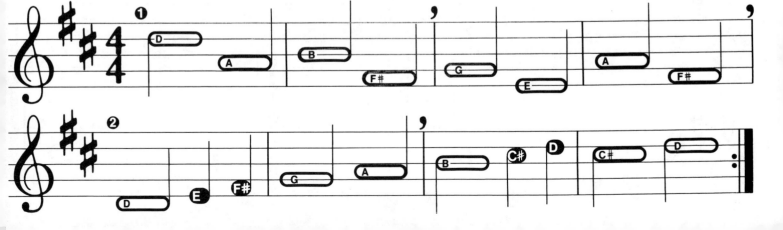

CHOPSTICKS DUET

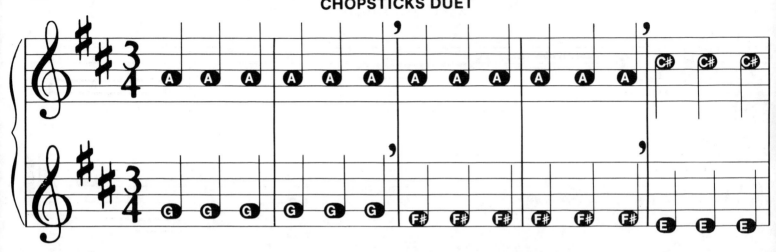

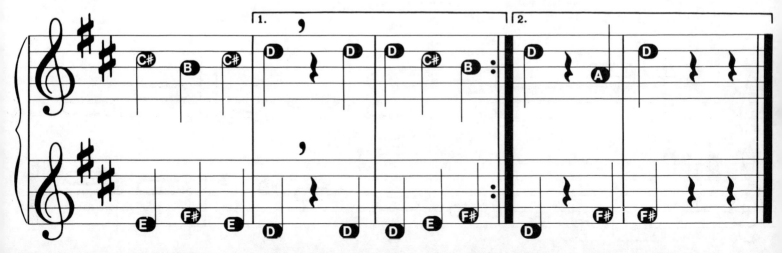

SWEET BETSY FROM PIKE

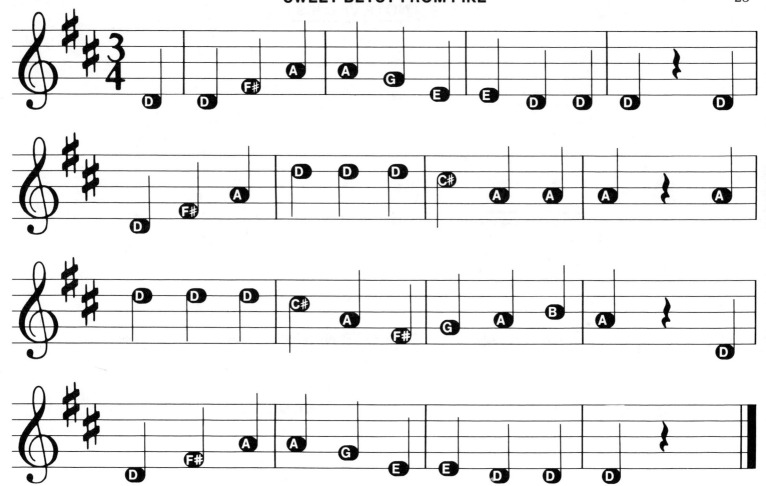

NOTE VALUES

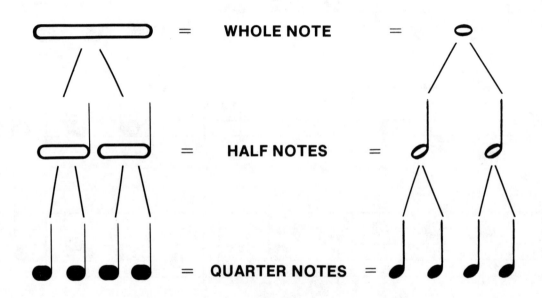

	=	WHOLE NOTE	=	
	=	HALF NOTES	=	
	=	QUARTER NOTES	=	

COUNT   1 + 2 + 3 + 4 +   COUNT   1 + 2 + 3 + 4 +

D E F# G A B C# D

JOLLY OLD SAINT NICHOLAS

Fill in note names: B

DOTTED HALF NOTE

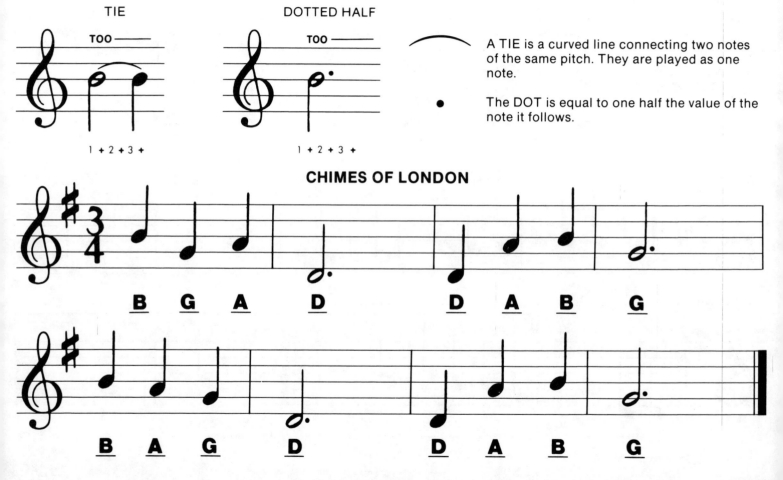

TIE

TOO ———

1 + 2 + 3 +

DOTTED HALF

TOO ———

1 + 2 + 3 +

A TIE is a curved line connecting two notes of the same pitch. They are played as one note.

The DOT is equal to one half the value of the note it follows.

CHIMES OF LONDON

B G A   D   D A B   G

B A G   D   D A B   G

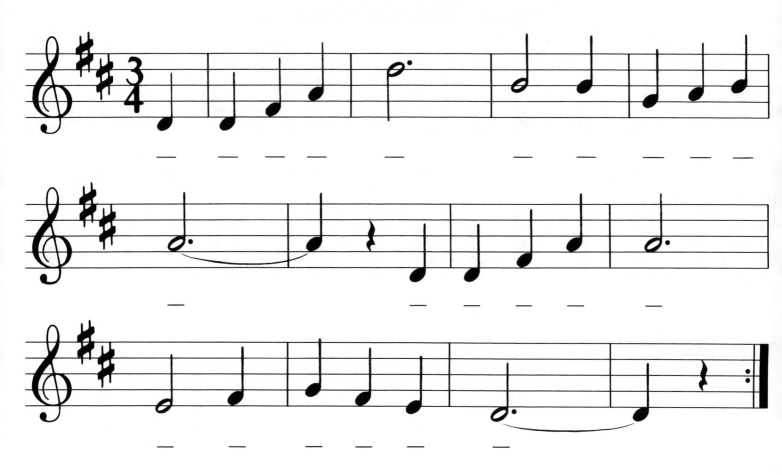

OH, HOW LOVELY IS THE EVENING (Round)

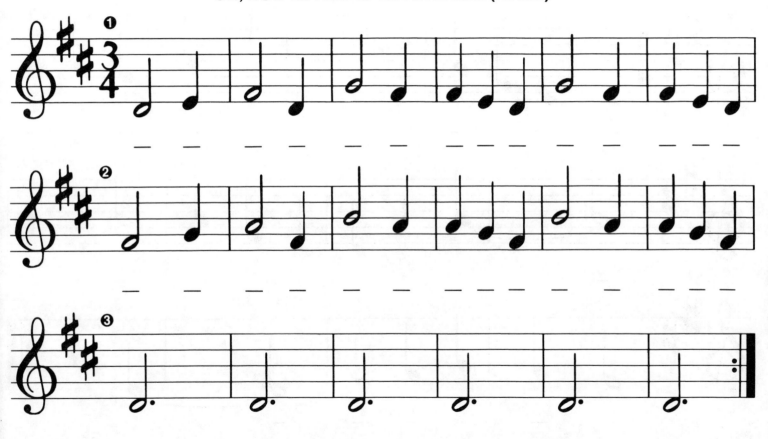

ROW, ROW, ROW YOUR BOAT (Round)

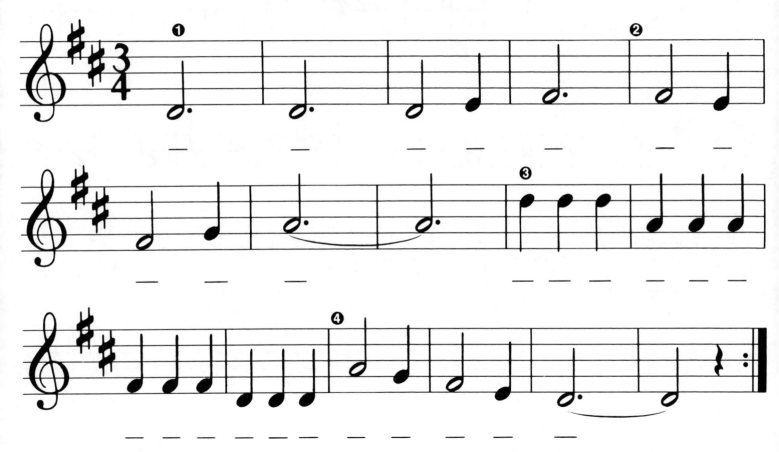

THREE BLIND MICE (Round)

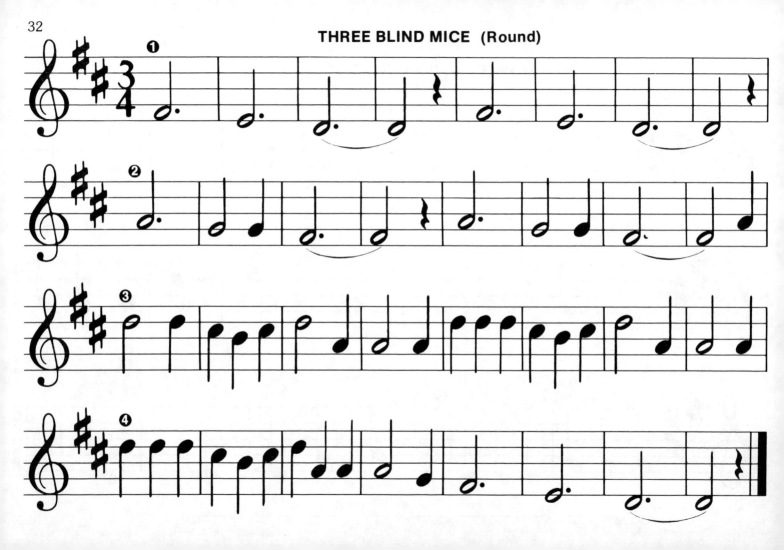

OVER THE RIVER

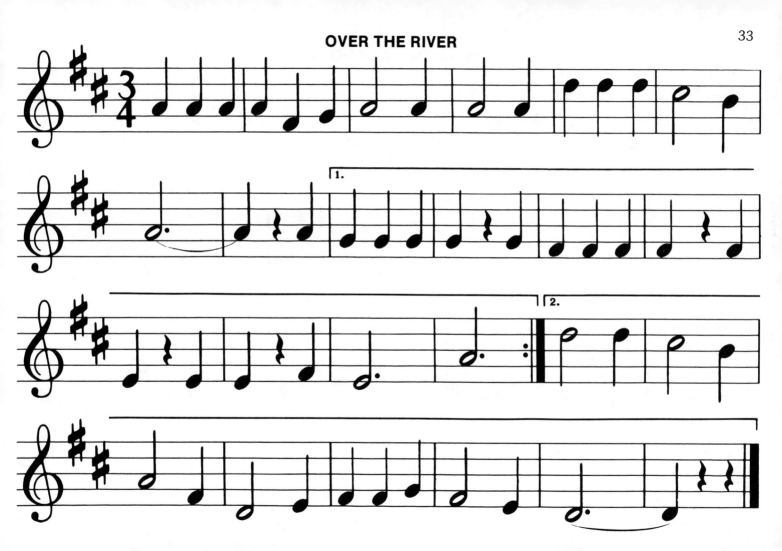

BLOW THE MAN DOWN

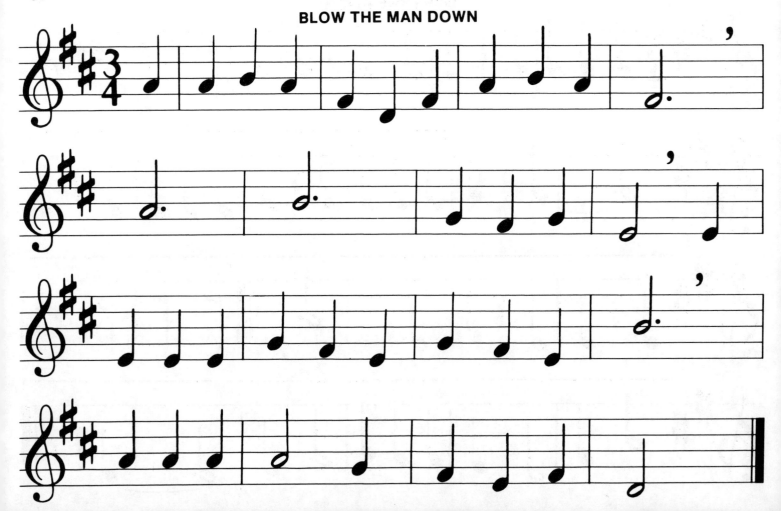

CARNIVAL OF VENICE

WHEN THE SAINTS COME MARCHING IN

SHE'LL BE COMIN' 'ROUND THE MOUNTAIN

NOTE VALUES

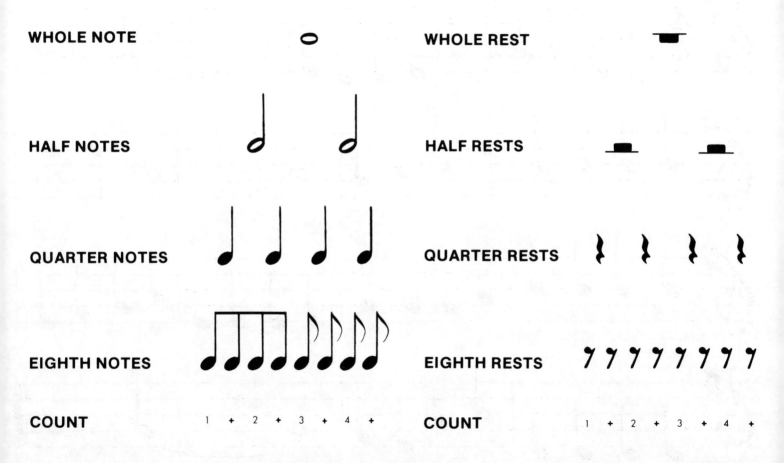

WHOLE NOTE	**WHOLE REST**
HALF NOTES	**HALF RESTS**
QUARTER NOTES	**QUARTER RESTS**
EIGHTH NOTES	**EIGHTH RESTS**
COUNT 1 + 2 + 3 + 4 +	**COUNT** 1 + 2 + 3 + 4 +

EIGHTH NOTES

The EIGHTH NOTE receives one half of a count and is written with one flag or connecting bar.

40

HUSH LITTLE BABY

LONG, LONG AGO

OLD MACDONALD HAD A FARM

BELLA BIMBA

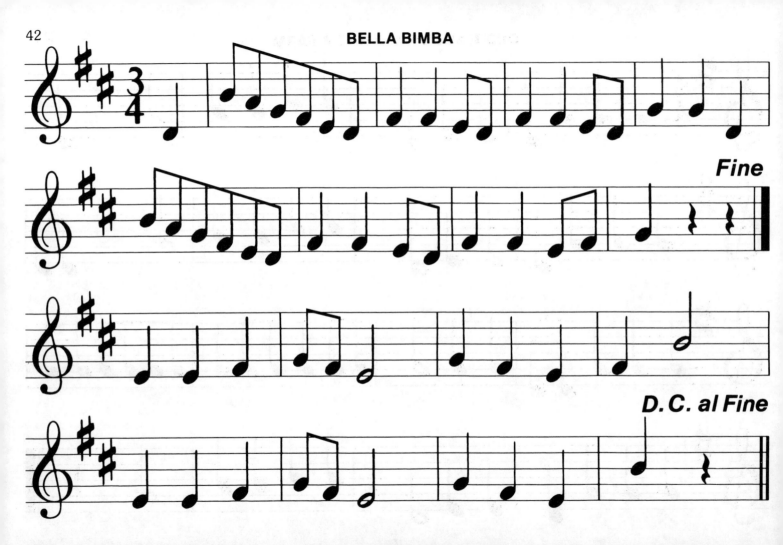

THE CANCAN

INDEX